When this book first made its appearance, Bob Dylan was the new kid on the block. A spectacular talent, but would it all last? Now, we know the answer. Dylan's unique gifts—his songs, writings and performances—have endured. He is part of our culture and part of our language. Journalists, educators, politicians, artists and writers around the world continue to recognize his contributions and draw from his work—new audiences find the magic—and the music goes on and on. These photographs were made during the sixties, a special and exciting time. I'm glad I was there—and able to preserve a piece of it. The original book was dedicated to Bob Dylan, and this one is too.

Dan Kramer

New York City

January 1991

Bob **Dylan** by Daniel Kramer

A Portrait of the Artist's Early Years

CITADEL UNDERGROUND

adel Press
blished by Carol Publishing Group
w York

For Arline

First Citadel Underground Edition 1991

A Citadel Press Book
Published by Carol Publishing Group
Citadel Press is a registered trademark of
Carol Communications, Inc.

Editorial Offices   Sales & Distribution Offices
600 Madison Avenue   120 Enterprise Avenue
New York NY 10022   Secaucus, NJ 07094

In Canada: Musson Book Company
A division of General Publishing Co. Limited
Don Mills, Ontario

Designed by Peretz Kaminsky

Manufactured in the United States of America

10 9 8 7 6 5 4 3 2 1

ISBN 0-8065-1224-5

Bob Dylan

Before the summer of 1963 if I were asked to name a folk song, I probably would have said "On Top of Old Smokey." If I were asked to name a folksinger, I probably would have been at a loss. I didn't know very much about folk music, and I didn't care. At the age of twelve, when I spent two weeks at a Boy Scout camp, I learned about blue-tail flies, herring boxes without topses, girls with long flaxen hair, mountain ranges, and little dogies who were getting along, and every now and then I would go through a few stanzas of "Streets of Laredo" if I happened to be sitting around a camp fire, or I would hum along with "Home on the Range" if I happened to run into that one, but I never pursued the matter further. It seemed to me that all of these songs were meaningless as far as their statements were concerned; they were just pleasant things to have around at a cook-out. The lyrics of one song were pretty much like the lyrics of another, and there seemed to be very little difference in the musical frameworks upon which these lyrics were hung. For the most part, I didn't see very much difference between this kind of music and the fairy tales of the Little Red Riding Hood and Jack and the Beanstalk variety. So I just let it all go by.

I successfully managed to stay removed until the summer of 1963, when a friend who was aware of my prejudice against this music urged me to watch the performance of a young folksinger appearing on a television program. I am convinced now that had I been looking for a TV show to watch and chanced upon this performance by Bob Dylan, hearing his voice would have been enough to catch me. It was the kind of sound I had always liked. It reminded me of a voice from the hills. It was an old voice, it seemed craggy and weatherbeaten, like a voice that had been left out in the rain and rusted. I attributed veracity to this voice because it sounded unprofessional—maybe that was what captured me. People who sound like that usually don't become singers. Dylan's sound made me look for something more.

There *was* something more. He was singing about the wanton slaying of an aging hotel maid by a young, wealthy, and influential guest at a Baltimore dinner party. As the story took shape, I realized that Dylan was singing about the corruption of justice. A newspaper account of the woman's murder inspired Dylan to write this song, called "The Lonesome Death of Hattie Carroll." He placed the corruption, named names, and concluded by insinuating that we were all responsible. He accompanied himself on the guitar, which he seemed more to "use" than to play in the conventional sense. The incessant strumming perfectly outlined and punctuated his message. It heightened at moments when he was delivering the strongest part of his material. It was like a tapping on my shoulder that said "Hey—listen! I have something very important to tell you." There was no getting away from it—I had to listen.

From time to time, he added to the overall effect by forsaking his lyric and playing the harmonica that hung about his neck in a wire holder. The music of the guitar was strong and pulsating and had a feeling that complemented the message of his song and emphasized its urgency. When he played the harmonica, it was another sound, another feel—more tender, more lilting. It was more the feeling of the slain woman, Hattie Carroll. The two instruments playing against each other gave musical dimension to his ideas and enabled me to experience the tragedy more deeply.

Part of what amazed me was the paradox of Dylan. On the screen I saw a young man with a sensitive, poetic face, yet the voice I heard was that of an older, more seasoned man. The general feeling he imparted, and the way he was dressed, suggested a backwoods country person, while the imagery and construction of his lyric were highly sophisticated. The lyric was tightly woven and pointed, his thoughts were fired straight at their mark. This sophistication seemed incongruous with his simple, natural appearance.

Hours later, when Dylan was no longer on the TV screen, I was still aware of his tapping on my shoulder. I was completely taken by what this man had done and how he had done it. His performance was perfect. With simple, basic tools—his voice, a guitar, and a harmonica—he drove his message deep into my mind. I felt that what he had done by telling me about this corruption of justice was not only perceptive but brave. This slight young man was doing what many of us feel we should be doing—speaking out. No one else that I was aware of was dealing with such material in this way. More than that, I was impressed by his performance: his face, his physical appearance, the total effect he produced. I was aware that I was seeing a very important talent. I wanted to photograph him so that others who hadn't heard of Bob Dylan would know of him and what he was doing. I wanted others to know what he was saying.

Unfortunately, it was not that simple. I knew almost nothing about folksingers, let alone how to find one, and my inquiries among friends who were folk music fans

drew blanks. The search was on—where can I find Dylan? Does he have an address? A phone? A someplace? He seemed to have none of these.

"Look around in the Village."

I did.

"Call this one."

I did.

"Call that one."

I did.

No Dylan.

I tried to get information about him, but always came up with the same few facts. He was born in Duluth, Minnesota, in May of 1941, grew up in Hibbing, Minnesota, left home in his teens, roamed the United States, and came to Greenwich Village about 1961. He had his first success at Gerde's Folk City in the Village, was well reviewed, wrote an important song of the times, "Blowin' in the Wind," and went on to his first important concert appearance at Town Hall in New York on April 12, 1963.

Eventually, someone told me that he was managed by Albert Grossman. I called the Grossman office. Everyone was very polite and understanding, but for one reason or another, Mr. Dylan was not available. I was asked to write a letter explaining who I was and what I wanted with Bob Dylan. The letter was sent. No answer. Weeks went by. No answer. I started the phone calls again. There was always a good reason for Dylan not being available, but there was no Dylan.

One evening when I least expected it, Mr. Grossman called me at my home. He informed me that arrangements could possibly be made when Bob was back in town, but at the moment he was in Europe. More waiting.

In August of 1964, exactly one year after I first saw Dylan perform, a date was set for a picture session. Arrangements were made for me to photograph him at the upstate home of his manager, where Dylan was resting and working on new material.

Finally.

The day I met Bob Dylan started with a two-hour drive to Woodstock, New York. Just beyond the town, set off from the public road by an unmarked driveway, and concealed from view by an expanse of grounds covered with trees and heavy foliage, is the home of Albert Grossman. A sign posted on a tree along the driveway reads: "If you have not telephoned, you are trespassing."

Here Dylan spent a good deal of his time when he was not on the road or in the city. More than a hideout, it was a peaceful retreat. The house was large and comfortable, the grounds well-kept. There was a pool behind the house, and two smaller buildings were used as a garage and guest house. Everything was bright and still on this warm August morning. It was a perfect place to separate from the world.

Dylan was not at home when I arrived, and I passed the time waiting for him at the pool. The quiet of the morning was broken by the roar of a motorcycle in the driveway. It disappeared into the garage, and moments later a thin, gangly young man dressed in bluejeans, boots, and a rumpled work shirt walked toward me. Ringlets of hair protruded from under his motorcycle rider's cap. His pale complexion and slight frame made him appear younger than the twenty-three years I knew him to be. As we greeted each other, we shook hands, and I was surprised at how gentle his handshake was. The feeling Dylan projected on the TV screen was one of strength. The mild handshake seemed to be out of character for this man, yet it made me think of the handshake of Floyd Patterson whom I met at the time of his reign as world heavyweight boxing champion. His handshake was also meek and mild, but I knew him to be a strong and powerful man. In both cases it was perplexing.

After we exchanged some words of greeting, I explained what I came to do—that I wanted to photograph him, to document him. Dylan said he had expected me. Although he was polite and friendly, he didn't seem to have much enthusiasm for making the pictures. As we spoke, he shuffled his feet and bobbed his head up and down somewhat impatiently, as though preoccupied. He told me he would be about the house and I should feel free to photograph him. People are usually eager to place themselves at the disposal of the photographer in order to make the pictures as effective as possible. They want to know how they can be helpful, asking where the photographer would like to work or what they should wear. They are willing to construct artificial situations. Dylan did not do this. Instead, he said he had some things to do, and excused himself.

What I wanted to do was to arrange and pose him in situations that would be revealing or symbolic. When I followed him into the house, I found him sitting at a dining booth in the kitchen reading a newspaper. He turned the pages of the newspaper and seemed never to acknowledge my presence. This set the pace. Apparently he was not going to do anything especially for the camera. It was not that he wasn't cooperating. Actually, he was being cooperative in his way—he allowed me to be with him, he allowed me to photograph him and to select my own pictures, as long as they derived from the situation I found him in.

At one point, after I had worked for a while and made a number of pictures, I suggested we go out to the front porch, where the light was very good. I asked him to sit in a rocking chair, which he did, but after a few moments he stood up, telling me this was not the way he would like to be photographed. I was aware, even on first acquaintance, that Dylan is a restless man. It is difficult to pin him down, difficult for him to remain still. It was also obvious that he didn't like to be photographed. He said that photography was a waste of his time and that he didn't want to pose. I stopped shooting and, there on the porch, explained what it was I wanted to do. I told him again what I felt the first time I saw him on the television screen a year before. I wanted him to cooperate so I could document who he was and what he was doing, and, I hoped, the pictures would eventually find their way to the public. He let me know he understood this and that he was willing to cooperate, but that he wanted the pictures to come from the things he did and not from things we would arrange for him to do. So I suggested photographing him doing the things which seemed most natural for him—working, writing music, or playing the guitar.

Dylan sat himself in a swing on the porch and told me that the pictures I wanted wouldn't work out, since he is always alone when he writes, and that it would be silly to make a picture of him posing at the typewriter. As for the guitar, he almost never played except when performing and he didn't like pictures with the instrument. Instead, he suggested I photograph him on the swing. His mood changed when he stood up and he pumped the swing higher and higher. He smiled—a rare thing, I learned, for Dylan to do for the camera. I felt I was being challenged and decided to meet it by not forcing the situation.

We were interrupted by Victor Maymudes, Dylan's road manager, a tall, dark-haired man with a strong face that I had seen many times in paintings of the Italian

Renaissance. Victor is a quiet man, who is acutely aware of everything around him. His job was to accompany Dylan to his concerts and manage the affairs necessary to bring about the night's performance. More than this, he was Bob's friend, and the two men often spent time together when they were not working. On this day, they spent some time playing chess at Bernard's Café Espresso in Woodstock, where we went for lunch.

Bernard's café is a wonderful place—a combination coffee house-restaurant-café. It has the qualities and charms of all three. I was introduced to Bernard, a large man both inside and out, who sported a broad mustache. Bob and Victor played chess at an outdoor table shaded from the sun by an overhanging roof. The red and white checkered tablecloths, some wine and cheese, the two men relaxing, made me feel we had all been transported to the local café of a quiet French village.

When we returned to the house, Bob and Victor spent some time practicing with bullwhips. I was surprised to see Dylan wielding his whip with great facility, cracking it in the air with an authority equal to Victor's, although Victor is a much larger man. I began to question the mild handshake I received as a greeting. Dylan was certainly not a weakling; on the contrary, he impressed me as being a strong, quick, active person. He was always on the move; even when sitting he was not still—there would usually be some movement: one foot beating time in the air, or a leg jiggling nervously. This is characteristic of Dylan, especially when he is forced to wait or sit for any length of time. If standing, he would often bend and straighten one leg to a steady pulsation, as if he needed an outlet for his energy. His restlessness keeps him on the move. This is an extension of the man himself. Dylan is always in flux. He is always on the move and what he produces is always on the move. I found this to be true after I came to know him better. He is constantly looking for new things and new ideas, and when he finds them, he bends them into a shape that is uniquely his own.

The light was beginning to fade. It was getting late and we decided to stop shooting. Dylan walked with me to my car in the gray light of a day's end. He asked me to let him know when the pictures could be seen. As we parted, we shook hands, and I couldn't help noticing that this handshake was firmer and warmer than the one he had greeted me with.

As I drove back to New York, I thought about the five hours I had spent with Dylan. They seemed to reveal some essential part of his personality. It was evident that he was a man who set his own marks and did not allow himself to be manipulated. He acted from his own convictions and took a stand. He knew what he wanted

to do and what he wanted to produce, and he went about it directly and with determination. He presents himself as he presents his work. He doesn't sell—it is up to you to meet it and extract from it. He forces nothing on you; if you want to deal with it, that is your own business. This was very much the way he handled the situation of being photographed.

The best way to photograph Dylan seemed to be to anticipate the pictures and not to force them. Pictures are always occurring and coming together in the natural environment and course of events. If the photographer can anticipate the actions and reactions of his subject and the subject's movements, he can bring together all of the elements before him to form his pictures. When pictures are made this way, they are often better than the posed variety. Certainly they are more truthful. Except for the making of album cover pictures and one rare studio sitting, all the photographs I took of Dylan were made using this method of anticipation. In one case, it made things a little more difficult; in another, it made the pictures a little more meaningful. Once we began to communicate and he realized that I was not out to alter him but was searching for interesting and significant pictures, he worked along more easily, allowing himself to enter into a number of situations that could lend interest to the photographs. We were able to work together.

The next time I saw Dylan was at the New York office of his manager. He and Albert Grossman pored over the pictures we had made and liked them. Bob got a big kick out of one of him sitting in a tree, perched on a branch, looking as if he belonged there. He jokingly told Albert he should sing from a tree at his next concert. Grossman, without cracking a smile, convinced Bob that the problem of transporting it would present too many complications.

Dylan suggested I accompany him to a concert coming up the following week. He felt a work situation would yield some interesting pictures. I gladly accepted his invitation.

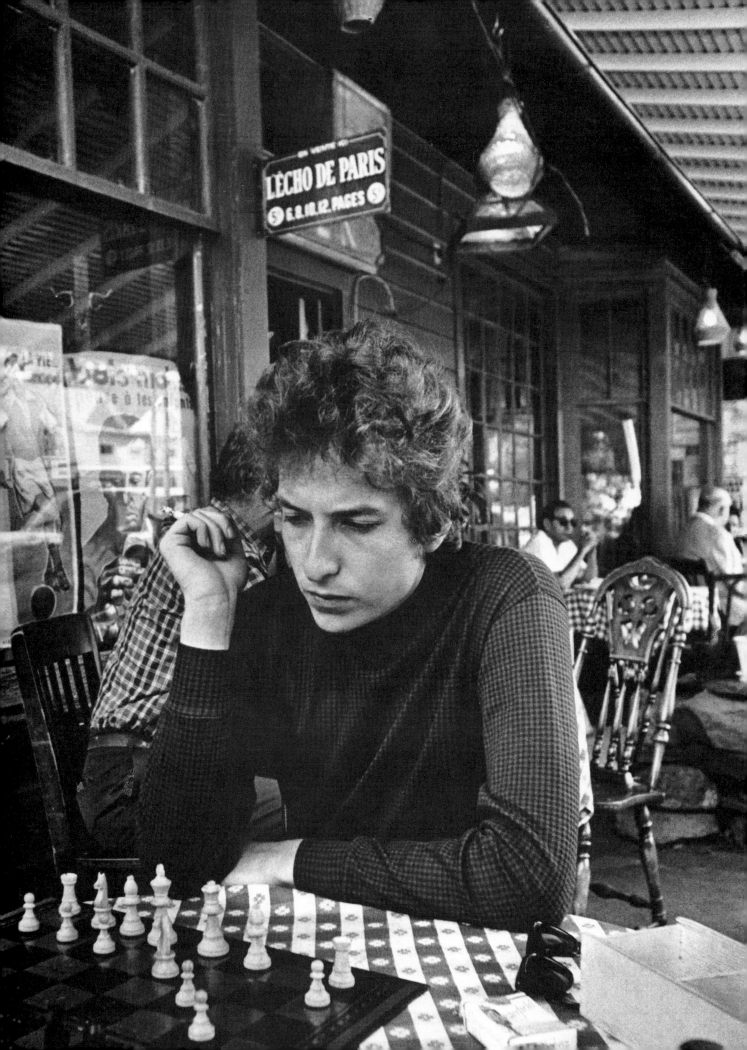

I didn't know when I began photographing Dylan that my association with him would become a long one, that I would photograph him not only once or twice or three times, but for a period of more than a year I would have the opportunity to document many facets of his life. I thought that after a few sessions I would have enough material to satisfy my needs. Instead, I learned that Dylan was more interesting and more exciting a subject than I expected—he was more than the little TV screen had allowed me to see. Dylan was changing and growing with each day. He was in a state of creative evolution. In just one year, not only his songs but his very appearance changed radically. He was new all the time. This is part of the phenomenon of Dylan. He tries not to be artistically in the same place twice—and he succeeds.

Dylan's appearance, his casual dress, the pile of hair on his head, and the legend of the folksinger as a free spirit led me to believe that his life was similarly carefree. I soon learned that his appearance is deceptive. That was obvious the first time I accompanied him to a concert and observed him meeting the challenges that are a part of a performer's life. I'm certain that most of the people who came to experience two hours of a Dylan concert were unaware of what effort, energy, and preparation were necessary to support and produce his performances.

It is not just a matter of performing on a stage; there is very much more to it. It means a great deal of time spent in travelling to and from concert locations, often a day or two just going and coming. For someone like Dylan, whose energy and creative abilities are constantly driving him, it is difficult to spend many hours sitting in a car, waiting at an airport, killing time in a hotel room. It isn't just the travelling; it means arriving at the location several hours before performance to prepare the microphones and test the stage lights, both time-consuming procedures. This is a necessary part of his work and, during the time I spent with him, he met the demands with an incredible degree of professionalism. He responded like a workman whose job was to go to a theatre somewhere, bringing his tools with him—his guitar, in an old battered case, several harmonicas, a small suitcase with his own microphones and connecting wires, and the clothes he would perform in. Victor Maymudes always accompanied him. Together, the two men would go off to their day's work, driving in Dylan's late model Ford station wagon, a little worse for wear. It meant a plane flight if the distance was greater than a hundred or so miles. A motel was usually the base of operations—a place to change, wash, and spend a few hours before the concert. Dylan avoided hotels whenever possible. He didn't want to deal with their lobbies and crowds of people.

The only playing he would do before the performance would be part of one or two songs so that the two mikes he used could be properly set—one for voice, placed a little below mouth-height, and a second at the height of the guitar. Finally, there was the time to be spent in the dressing room with nothing to do but wait for concert time.

What was obvious about Dylan was his ability to make the best use of any time he could extract from a day already crowded with things to do. When we met on the morning of our first trip, he seemed to be preoccupied. He was cordial and friendly, but asked Victor to drive about the city before departing. He didn't want to go anywhere in particular—he said he just wanted to clear his head. He seemed to be deep in thought. Maybe it had something to do with going to a concert, or maybe he needed the time to work out a new idea. He would grab at moments that were available to him, often writing in a small black looseleaf notebook, in which he probably wrote new material or kept ideas. He would interrupt something in order to glimpse a TV screen to see another performer. I've seen him use ten minutes working out melodies on a backstage piano while someone was out locating the key to his dressing room. He spent a great deal of time writing new material. At this, he was prolific. And there were always miscellaneous things, a TV show, or business to be conducted at the office of his manager.

Although these things consumed a great deal of his time, he tried hard to reserve some time for himself to do the things he felt like doing. He told me that one of the ways he manages to be punctual and accomplish things was to commit himself only to one or two things a day. In this way, he was able to meet the demands he placed upon himself. If he told me he would call on Thursday, I was pretty sure that I would get that call. In all such regards, he was reliable if he had agreed to a schedule. On the other hand, if he didn't want to be found, you couldn't find Bob Dylan.

After the equipment was tested, Bob would change into his performing clothes, which at the time consisted of suede boots, pressed denim jeans, usually a turtleneck shirt, and a favorite old suede jacket that was worn and stained. Somewhere along the line the jacket was lost, and he replaced it with another that looked very similar. Not quite the same, but similar. I think he felt that the old jacket was a lucky one.

He told me that in the early days of his career, when he had first come to New York, things were very difficult. It was hard to find work and money was scarce. It was true that sometimes he didn't have other clothes to change into, and that sometimes he went without bathing. The writers and reporters continued to write about this, he said, as if it was still a part of his life. It was not. But it was good copy for them, so they didn't let it go.

Frequently, friends would drop by the dressing room, often bringing wine. Bob never seemed to be ruffled, worried, or insecure. He always approached the concert as the "thing" he was doing—and it appeared very natural that he was doing that thing. Although there were always problems to be faced, he never created any. The only demands he made were the ones necessary for him to produce his work. The most reliable thing about his performances was his performance; the variations were usually in everything else—perhaps a sound problem in one auditorium or a lighting problem in another. He would usually spend some time alone a few minutes before the performance would start. But he never asked me to leave or asked me not to photograph. He never inhibited my working. There were times when I went out on the stage and photographed from behind him while he was performing, in order to get back shots, rim-lit by the spotlight. Standing in the darkness behind Dylan, I was able to feel the lonesome task he has every time he faces an audience. Once I asked him if I disturbed him when I put the camera up close while he performed. (I would crawl down the aisle, sneak up in front of the stage, and come within a few feet of him with my camera.) He said it didn't bother him because he couldn't see anything out there anyway. Considering the fact that his eyes are weak and he needs glasses to see well, the spotlight probably blinds him. Sometimes before a concert he would ask me about the age of his audience— if there were any older people out there. Older people were not people in their 60's, but people in their 30's. It pleased him when they came to hear him.

The travelling, the inconveniences, the waiting, the time spent and energy involved had one main objective—the concert itself. It would begin with Dylan waiting in the darkness of the wings for a cue to go on. He would stride out to the microphone and almost before he took his first step, he was met by the spotlight that escorted him to the center of the stage. He would start strumming his guitar before he reached the mike, as if he couldn't contain himself. This set the pace, creating a feeling of urgency, as if to say, there's hardly enough time—there's hardly enough time to get it all said —to get it all out. Once I asked him which songs he was going to sing. He said the problem was not which ones to perform but which ones to leave out. He wanted to do them all. He wanted to get it all said.

It surprised me that Dylan's young audiences were always attentive and quiet. They leaned forward, they wanted to hear. I think some of it had to do with the fact that they wanted to hear his material, but what was also obvious was that Dylan himself had captured them. He is that kind of performer. Whether it's natural talent, or produced effect, or whatever, Dylan has it. Alone, with just his guitar and harmonica, without physical gyrations, without beguiling little speeches, without any of the obvious show business attitudes, Bob was able to captivate and control an audience completely for two hours. I watched him do this concert after concert. His slightly bowed stance, outlined by the one spotlight, the pounding of his guitar or rhythmical strumming, the lilting runs on the harmonica, or its staccato-like punctuating, consistently, time after time, revealed that Dylan is a superlative performer. It is not a question of whether he is a great guitar player, or a harmonica virtuoso, or whether we agree that his voice is this, or is that, or is not this—he produces a total effect which always wins his audience.

I once stood in the back of a theatre in Buffalo, talking with a policeman who was there to control the crowds. He leaned over to me in the darkness and said, "He sings about some kind of philosophy, doesn't he? He's not like the others we've had here. The kids seem to listen to him—they're very quiet tonight. I don't have any problems with his audience. Last week, we had a guy in here with a guitar who just went crazy."

When Dylan appeared on the Les Crane television show, the workmen and stagehands, who had dismissed him as a curiosity during rehearsal, listened raptly once he began to sing. Later, putting down his guitar, he went on to charm, beguile, and confuse the show's host and audience—in a brand-new role as television personality talker. It happened over and over again—Dylan got to the people. They listened to him.

Although I attended many Dylan concerts, and heard many of the songs again and again, the commitment with which he performed always gave them a new life, and I often felt I was hearing and seeing Dylan for the first time. Sometimes, carried along by the musical excitement, my finger would depress the camera firing button as if it were a musical instrument, and I found myself photographing to the tempo of Dylan's playing.

When the performance was over, there was usually a wait in the dressing room while the crowds filed out, so that not more than a few dozen fans would stay for autographs, to talk with him, to touch him. Often when we left the theatre, we were pursued by other cars. Some of the more zealous fans would tail us, and it became like something out of an old grade B mystery movie. Perhaps the motive was to find out where Dylan was staying. Perhaps it was just a way of being playful. But Victor is an excellent driver and experienced at the game. He would shut off his headlights and swing into a parking lot, hide in a closed gas station, or slip through a changing traffic light. No one ever caught him.

The atmosphere after the concerts became an indication of the excitement being generated around Dylan. In a few months' time, it changed from dozens waiting at a stage door to hundreds crushing each other to reach him. The excitement for Dylan was growing with each day, and leaving the concert halls was becoming a challenge in itself. Once after a concert we waded through a heavy crowd and got into a car—but that's as far as it went. We were completely surrounded. Faces and hands were pressed against the windows. It was like a fishbowl, but you couldn't tell who was looking in and who was looking out. There was bumping on the sides, pounding on the roof, and the car began to rock. Bob's window was rolled down a little, and he was signing autographs. For a moment it was frightening. You never knew when a hand might come crashing through the plate glass. Finally, enough of a clearing was made and Victor was able to ease the car through the driveway out into the street. Dylan was becoming a star.

It seems that the calm that was upon Bob before a concert took on a restless quality when the day's work was over. He was seldom able to quit when his work was done. He would often look for something to do—a gathering of people, perhaps. He enjoyed going out to a late-night bar, drinking wine, meeting people there—relaxing, releasing, before he was ready to call it a night. Sometimes Dylan would spend time in the dressing room giving interviews, but only a few of the many requests for them were granted. He told me that no matter how hard he tried, the articles written about him never worked out—somewhere along the line they became distorted or inaccurate. Dylan would often answer reporters in a way that would make it obvious he felt the questions were silly or naive. He was asked by one reporter, "What do you really want to do?" Go to college, learn to make money, and be a success, he told her.

It was always the youngest interviewers who had the best chance. Dylan seemed to have the most patience with these people. Once after a concert at Princeton, to which Allen Ginsberg, a very enthusiastic fan and friend, had come, Dylan granted interviews first to a high school girl and then to a young man who was reporting for the first time for his college newspaper. The young man was well prepared with a list of questions, obvious ones, and Dylan, in his characteristic way, side-stepped, parried, joked, and in his usual fashion of being somewhat cryptic, spoke about meaningful things. The young man concluded with questions about the song "With God on Our Side." He asked Dylan, "Do you believe in what you say in that song?" "Do you believe in the words you write?" he asked. Dylan replied, I believe in every breath I take —and with that he embraced him and exclaimed,—and I believe in every breath you take! With this, Ginsberg, wearing a crown he found in the dressing room, embraced both of them and cried out, And I believe in every breath we ALL take! The reporter was a little shaken when the interview resumed, and Ginsberg, noticing this, offered to help by taking the pencil and pad from his hands and continuing the questioning. All in all, the fellow got some pretty good material.

On the way back to New York, we stopped at a diner for some late supper. I wouldn't say we were a strange-looking crew—Ginsberg, a huge scarf wrapped around his neck; a young poet friend of his with hair down to his shoulders; a girl dressed in what looked like an old theatrical costume; Dylan with his wild hair, and myself with a beard I wore at that time—but after we were seated, a woman came over to our table and asked if we had just come from a masquerade party. We told her we had, and she left satisfied, believing that all was still right with the world.

It was inevitable that the particular talents of Bob Dylan and Joan Baez would find their way to one stage. They performed together at the Newport Folk Festival. Then, on several occasions, Bob announced to his audience he would like to bring out a friend, and the friend would appear in the person of Joan Baez. He also would appear unannounced at concerts she gave, and eventually several joint Dylan-Baez concerts were produced in major cities. These shared programs were often more than just a combination of the two performers—a third entity emerged, producing an overwhelming effect. At times, in order to accommodate the material or the sound they produced together, Dylan would sing in a voice he did not ordinarily use. It was sweeter, softer.

Sometimes he would forsake the wire harmonica holder he wore about his neck and hand-hold the instrument in order to get the effects necessary to accompany Joan's voice. The rapport they generated with the audience was tremendous. At one performance, by the time the concert was half over, most of the people in the rear of the theatre had left their seats and filled the aisles and the area in front of the stage. They sat on the carpeted floor of the theatre, packed shoulder to shoulder, so that it was impossible for me to move about and make pictures. The audience showed more than enthusiasm; this was warmth, understanding, and love.

I remember a night after a Dylan-Baez concert in Buffalo. The crowd had been particularly hectic, and we got away from the theatre only by making a great effort not to run down the fans who had collected about the car. We drove past a young blond girl standing on the curb holding a Dylan album in her hand—one that Bob had autographed for her earlier. Tears streamed down her face as we pulled away. Later, after we had out-run our pursuers and were heading for the motel, someone began talking about the girl—the expression on her face, her tears, her silence, the way she just stood there. It was compelling. Joan suggested we go back and find her and invite her to join us. The risk was that we would be noticed by crowds still milling about. It had been a long day and everyone was weary, but Bob decided we should chance it, go back and look for the girl. We did. We drove back to the theatre. Most of the crowd had already left. We looked about, we even asked some people if they had seen a blond girl about fourteen years old, but no, no one had seen her—then, yes, someone said, she went down that street. We drove down that street, but we never found her. I think we all felt as sad as she might have felt had she known we were looking for her. (Anyway, little blond girl, I thought you would like to know.)

In late winter, Dylan and Joan Baez gave a joint concert at Convention Hall in Philadelphia. Ten thousand people filled this enormous place. As I roamed through the auditorium, photographing from different vantage points, I came at one time to the last row in the last balcony. All I could see far below me was a tiny circle of light in which was a figure I could barely identify as Dylan. It was amazing that people sitting this far from the stage responded as if they were in the tenth row—absorbed, attentive, yet getting Dylan's voice from a nearby loudspeaker. I asked myself the questions I had been asked many times: Why do they come? What is the magic of Dylan? I had a clue some weeks earlier when I heard him rehearse a few songs in a small dressing room in the basement of a theatre. There, in that tiny room, Dylan

was as moving and as exciting as he is on a concert stage. Yet he produced this effect without an audience, without a spotlight, without any of the embellishments of a performance. The answer seemed to be that he didn't need any of these things in order to produce that which is Dylan. The only place left to look was in the man himself. There I found three elements coming together at once that make him so compelling. Dylan perceives relationships in his environment beyond those held up for him to see, and, in so doing, has sidestepped the mold society would have pressed him into. Secondly, he is endowed with the ability and artistry necessary to arrange and blend these insights into whole structures that reveal to us what he sees. And as a talented and effective performer, he is totally capable of delivering his material to us in a highly personal and dramatic way. Since Dylan alone is responsible for the entire creation, and it goes through no other interpretative process, nothing is lost and we are able to get close to his original insight. Dylan is a *self-contained unit of communication,* capable of delineating the experiences of his generation with his words.

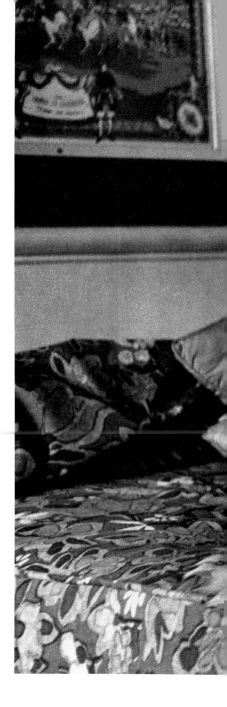

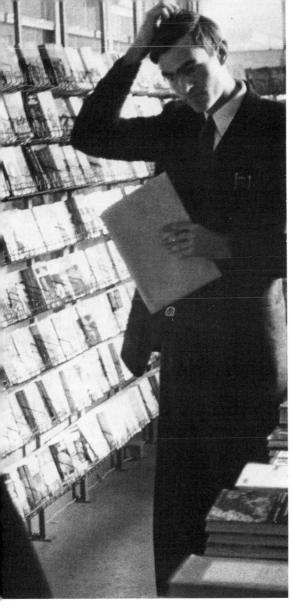

The poet, the writer, the creator of ideas has always been around. He is often shaped and molded by the moment in which he lives, or the medium of communication at his disposal. He first chiseled on a cave wall, later he wrote on parchment, of which only one or a few copies would be available, and finally it was a book printed by the thousands. There were times when the poet may have been a wandering troubadour, his instrument slung on his back, the road before him. In other times, Dylan might have been the wandering troubadour, but today there are record companies, and that changes everything. A combination of the new technology of the record and the old need for man to express himself, to create, to communicate ideas, has brought about a new and powerful means of expression. Now it may be that the poet will use a new medium of communication, the phonograph record, and Bob Dylan may well be the man that established this medium as a place for the poet.

What is unique about the phonograph record is that one copy of it travelling over the airways can reach millions of people at once. Even those who cannot read are susceptible to it. It takes less than three minutes to play the average recorded song. It can be heard on a car radio, it can be played on a record player for many people at a gathering, it can be listened to on a tiny transistor radio carried in a shirt pocket. If the message is backed up by and set in the framework of a contemporary musical form, it draws the young people to it—while the music runs through them, the message can run into them. Advertising companies know this and feed us messages about soft drinks backed up by a rock beat. Lyrics and music were recorded before Bob Dylan was born. What Bob Dylan brought to the popular record was a meaningful lyric. His lyrics, his message, may well be the most significant change in popular music in the last few hundred years. When the idea contained in a song such as "Blowin' in the Wind" is expressed in a literary magazine, it goes just so far. When it is recorded, it reaches millions of young people at a most impressionable age. It can change the way they think. It can motivate them to act. When "Blowin' in the Wind" blew throughout the world on the wings of a phonograph record, it carried a charged message of our times.

The first time I attended a Dylan recording session was in January of 1965 at Studio A in the Columbia Records building at 799 Seventh Avenue in New York City. Bob had retired to Woodstock to write new material for an album, and when he walked into the session two weeks later he brought eighteen new songs with him. The record was eventually titled "Bringing It All Back Home." His entire career had been punctuated with variations upon his existing work, but for this album he was going to strike out in a new direction. Except for "Corina, Corina" in the "Freewheelin' Bob Dylan" album, and perhaps another rare occasion, Bob had always recorded alone. But now he was going for a new sound, and Tom Wilson, his recording producer, started a search for musicians who could work with him. It was crucial to use musicians who could really play, who could accommodate Dylan's needs. Musicians not used to playing with him would have to adjust to his unorthodox style and method of delivery—if he had something important to say in a lyric, he might unexpectedly slow down the tempo, then rush on to the next thing until he had something else he wanted to emphasize, then slow down again, fitting the music to his messages. Playing alone, Dylan could have great impact doing this, but it was difficult for other players to anticipate what he was going to do. Not only did these musicians need to be experienced players, they had to be sensitive, and flexible, and open to changing an idea, or abandoning one, in the course of producing the music. Just as it happens in the making of the best jazz music, it happened right there in Studio A on the spot.

It was obvious from the very beginning that something exciting was happening, and much of it happened spontaneously. When the playback of "Maggie's Farm" was heard over the studio speakers, we were all elated. There was no question about it—it swung, it was happy, it was good music, and, most of all, it was Dylan. The musicians were enthusiastic. They conferred with one another to work out the problems as they arose. Dylan bounced around from one man to another, explaining what he wanted, often showing them on the piano what was needed until, like a giant puzzle, the pieces would fit and the picture emerged whole. Dylan worked like a painter covering a huge canvas with the colors that the different musicians could supply him, adding depth and dimension to the total work. All in all, most of the songs went down easily and needed only three or four takes before they were accepted. In some cases, the first take sounded entirely different from the final one because the material was played at a different tempo, perhaps, or a different chord was chosen, or solos may have been re-arranged. As the sound was created, the word seeped out, and more and more people began to visit during the sessions. At times the control room looked like a commuter train packed with people watching the scenery. During the playbacks, we danced and sang to the music. It was a party of sound and music—there was wine, sandwiches, and a lot of hard work.

Dylan moved through it all with enthusiasm, calculating, dealing with the ideas, exchanging his concepts with the other players. They all gave to the creation, communicating and contributing their individual talents.

At one point Dylan lost his temper. He had been asked to sing into a microphone that was placed in front of two baffle panels arranged by the engineer to control the sound quality. Without Dylan's knowledge, Tom Wilson had arranged an "obstacle course" around the mike area, consisting of music stands, mike stands, and other paraphernalia, placed in such a way as to inhibit Dylan from moving around the studio or wandering off and leaving the microphone area. This wall of equipment finally got on his nerves; he felt closed in and distracted by it. He suddenly stopped singing and bellowed over the microphone, "Can't we get rid of some of these things? Let's start with this"—and he grabbed a chair that was placed a few feet in front of him, lifted it, and ran halfway across the studio with it. After putting it down, he turned toward the control booth, smiled, then broke into a laugh, realizing it was not necessary to be upset. All he needed to do was ask to have the floor cleared. He did, and it was.

I discovered that Dylan is a much better musician than he usually allows people to realize. In order to meet the challenges that grew out of the recording session, I saw him call more and more upon his musical ability and his technical knowledge, and this helped him win the respect and cooperation of the other musicians. Someone who has worked closely with him told me he wouldn't be surprised at anything Bob did. If Dylan could play the violin, he said, you might not hear it until ten years from now —as happened when Dylan surprised everyone by playing the piano in recent recording and in-person performances.

Between takes, Dylan would work individually with the musicians until he was satisfied with what was happening. He was patient with them and they were patient with him. His method of working, the certainty of what he wanted kept things moving. He would listen to the playbacks in the control booth, discuss what was happening with Tom Wilson, and move on to the next number. If he tried something that didn't go well, he would put it off for another session. In this way, he never bogged down—he just kept on going.

At the next to last session, Dylan recorded "Tambourine Man," "It's All Right, Ma," and "Gates of Eden" one after the other, without hearing a playback. He had tried "Tambourine Man" a day earlier but set it aside because it didn't work out. This day he announced that he didn't want the engineering booth to goof—that these were long numbers and that he didn't want to do them more than once. They were recorded just that way, in one take.

A funny thing happened on the way to recording "Bob Dylan's 115th Dream." He was to start playing the acoustical guitar and, at a certain point, the other musicians were to join in. For some reason, the other players missed their cue and Dylan started singing anyway, almost as if he was not used to the idea that other instruments would accompany his. He was just playing. He was doing his thing. It took him a moment to realize they had not come in with him and he had gone on ahead. Dylan began to laugh. Tom Wilson broke up in hysterical laughter, and soon everyone in the studio was caught up in it. Bob insisted that this laughter be kept on the final track for the release of the album. He shouted into the mike to Tom Wilson that he would even be willing to pay for it. The laughter was kept in the recording. Since Dylan's success with this release, I've been told that a number of recording groups keep a "live" microphone on all the time during their sessions, hoping to get a planned "spontaneous" happening.

The number of takes piled up—experiments were made, solutions were found. Something new, created out of old parts, was being born in Studio A. Later it would be called Folk Rock, and it would permeate the entire world of popular music. Others would begin to record this sound, people would speculate on whether or not Dylan was true to himself when he produced it, lines would be drawn, stands would be taken. But on this day, when it all happened, it was a matter of excellent musicians and a creative mind making music.

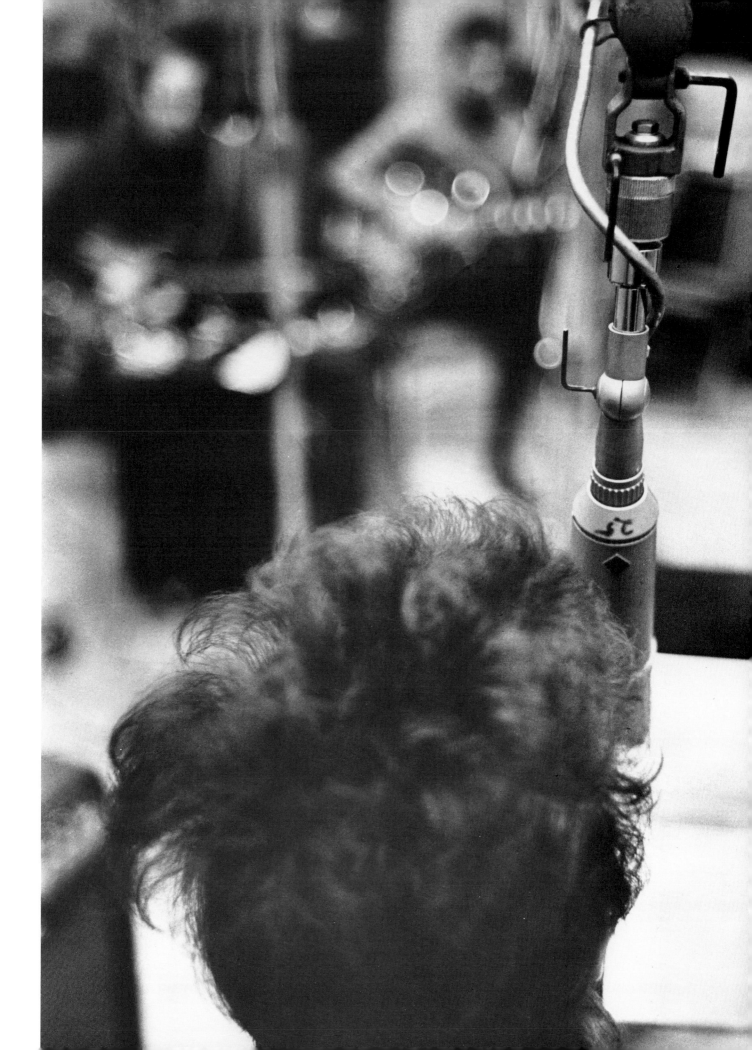

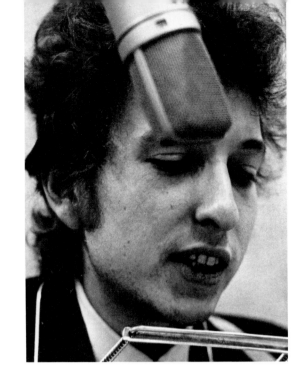

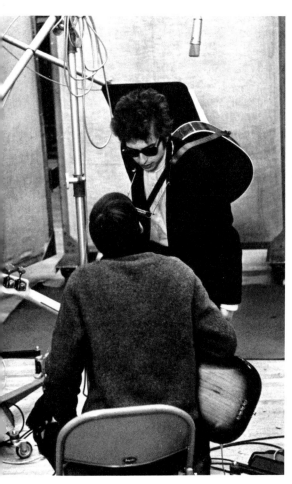

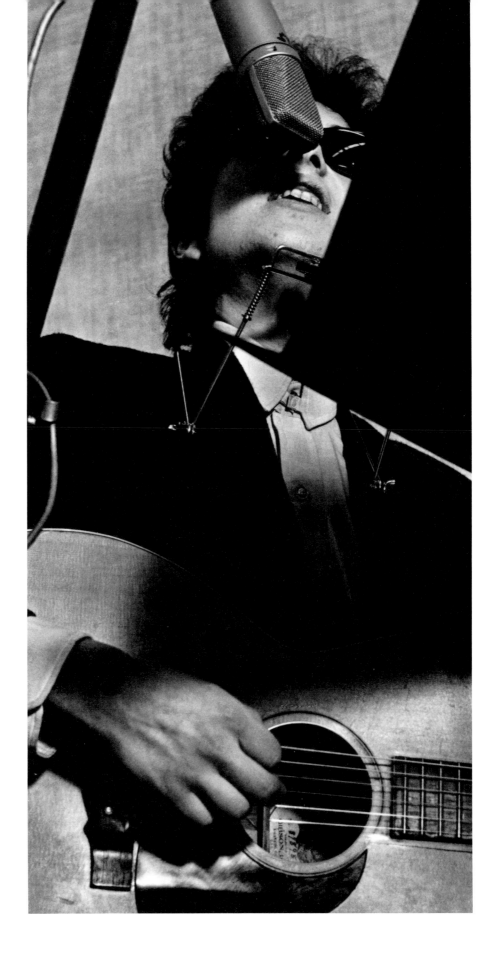

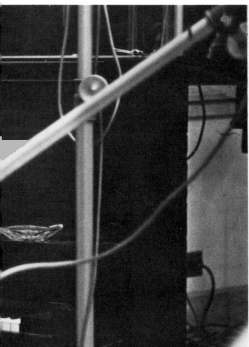

Dylan spent a good deal of his time in Woodstock and suggested that we make the album cover picture for "Bringing It All Back Home" there. It was mid-winter. The city was covered with snow. Under almost blizzard conditions, Bob, a careful driver, drove us to the country in his station wagon. We made our first stop in Woodstock—Bernard's Café. Blanketed with snow, its windows frosted over by the heat of an open hearth fire in the middle of the dining room, the café was different from the one I had visited on the warm August day I first met Dylan, when he and Victor played chess at an outdoor table. On this day we could hardly wait to get inside.

As on other occasions, we had dinner and talked. Bob spoke about his life before he came to New York City, when he spent some time with a circus. No one, he told me, has a more difficult existence than circus people, especially the "freaks"—the sideshow people and the geeks. You can learn a lot from them, he said. They are down and by some standards of society, they are very low on the social scale, yet they have found a way to make it, as if they understand some things about life that other people don't easily get a chance to learn. He seemed very fond of the circus and the people who worked in it. There are lines in his poetry and places in his songs where he alludes to the circus or to the image of the clown. In liner notes for a Joan Baez album, he uses the image of a saddened clown to describe himself at one moment in his youth. The imagery of the clown and the circus can be found in any number of places in his songs and his writings. With pieces of colored cut glass, glued to a sheet of clear glass, Bob once made the face of a clown and gave it to Bernard, who keeps it on display in his restaurant. It was lent to us the day we made the album cover for "Bringing It All Back Home." It can be seen in the photograph above the mantel, looking down on the scene below it. Once, after a concert at Princeton University, he joshed with his friend Allen Ginsberg that someday he would like to have a circus of his own. Ginsberg said he would like to be a part of it, and Dylan told him he would certainly be included.

Sometimes we spoke about more abstract things. Dylan told me that the future was too uncertain to plan for. Too many variables—including death—prevent us from considering the future as a certainty. He said that this was part of his philosophy and was reflected in the way he lived, more for the moment and the day than for tomorrow. I pointed out that although this was a part of his philosophy, it did not prevent him from dealing with the world of tomorrow, since his concert schedule, set in advance, was always met; his business and performing obligations were treated with a high degree of responsibility.

For several days, I had worked at conceiving an idea for the album cover. I wanted the picture to relate strongly to Dylan and to the feeling of the music that had been recorded. Although I spent a good deal of time searching for the picture, it didn't come together and solidify until the morning we began work. I explained the concept to Dylan and, as soon as I was able to, showed him a test polaroid picture of the idea. He like it and was excited by it. We worked much differently on this day than we had on the day of our first meeting. There was communication between us, and we were both able to work toward the same objectives. Bob enjoyed searching the house for props to be used, and helped in their arrangement. We spent most of the day this way, designing the set. I made some polaroid pictures to test my idea of making the background and props "move" around Dylan in the photograph. We were all excited by them. This was a far cry from the first picture session I had with him. Unlike his attitude the first time I photographed him, Bob posed under very difficult conditions, and accepted all the directions from behind the camera. Sally Grossman, the charming wife of Albert Grossman, who appears in the photograph, helped out by similarly enduring several hours of direction.

Time and time again, I asked Dylan to come to my studio so that I could photograph him in a controlled situation and make "the definitive portrait." Time and time again, he put me off. Finally I appealed to his sense of reason, and he agreed to come. I asked him to sit on a stool and do nothing but look into my camera. He did at first, but again he wasn't happy. It was the old rocking chair story; he didn't like to pose. He found his "swing"—his way of not dealing directly with the camera—by playing with things he found around the studio—holding a dart board, carrying my camera case, holding a coffee cup or an ashtray, draping himself with a big black cloth—posing with obviously *made* expressions. Instead of sitting on the stool, he put one foot up on it and half-hid his face with his right hand. He was physically doing what he felt—he was hiding from the camera. Yet he was smiling out from behind his hand, as if he knew what was going on. He was playing the way he played with interviewers and reporters; the way he sometimes plays with the whole world. This is the picture I used for my book cover. This, for me, depicts the many Dylans in one.

Eventually, photography became something that Dylan enjoyed. One day he called and asked me if I wanted to take some pictures. Fifteen minutes later he arrived at my studio with his friends, Peter Yarrow, of Peter, Paul and Mary, and

John Hammond, Jr., the folksinger, and suggested we go out to the street and have some fun. Another time, in Woodstock, he borrowed one of my cameras and photographed me. It became a Western shoot-out, with each of us trying to "catch" the other with our cameras.

Bob wanted to make a picture for the cover of his book *Tarantula,* and again suggested we work in Woodstock. This time we used as a background an old shack. Trying to capitalize on the success of the album cover, we arranged props around Bob, most of them found in the shack. Unfortunately, we capitalized too well. The picture was so similar to "Bringing It All Back Home" that we decided not to use it. Bob wanted Sarah Lownds with him in this picture. Sarah, a dark-haired, attractive, soft-spoken woman, later became Mrs. Dylan. They now have a son, Jesse Byron Dylan.

In the course of more than a year, I never saw Dylan living in a place that was totally his own. He spent most of his time at the home or apartment of his manager. His possessions there besides his clothing were very few. There were times when he stayed at the home of a friend or at a hotel, where he had little more than his clothes with him. Freedom and the ability to strike out anywhere at any time are precious to him. He doesn't want to take on weight that might slow him down. Yet, it doesn't seem to hamper his ability to work and produce. He was able to work on *Tarantula* at several of the places where he was staying. He did most of his work in the country, but when he was in the city, he would re-organize, and work there. When he is involved with something, he concentrates on it. It's foremost in his mind, and he seems not to care about other things. Before he left on a concert tour of England, something he was looking forward to and was very excited about, he told me he was making believe that the concerts he was playing here in the States between then and the time of his departure, didn't exist. Although he was aware of them, and prepared to perform at each one, he was not considering them as part of his life—as if they were getting in his way, keeping him from doing something that was more important to him.

He is quite capable of working within restrictions when it is required. When several pages of my pictures were to be used in *Pageant,* Bob offered to write some lines of poetry for them. I went up to Woodstock with a layout of the picture story, and showed him the spaces allotted for the poetry. Each line could only have a set number of words. He took the layout, went to his room, and within an hour had produced poetry to accompany nine pages of pictures, each line fitting exactly the allotted space.

Dylan's career was moving at breakneck speed. With each week his stature grew, and the demands made on him increased. There were times when he was overwhelmed by this success. One night, while we sat in Gerde's Folk City, Bob told me that just two years before, when his career was beginning, he earned $90.00 a week there. Now he realized he could probably earn that much just by touching Gerde's wall. Giants in Dylan's own world of music were recognizing his talent. Pete Seeger, travelling in over twenty countries on a world tour, introduced Dylan the composer to new audiences by performing Dylan's "Who Killed Davey Moore?" Johnny Cash drove out to Trenton, New Jersey, to spend some time with Dylan. Although he could not arrive in time for Bob's concert, the two men drove back to New York in Cash's limousine listening to Johnny's latest record album on a transistor record player. The album included a Dylan song.

Yet, regardless of what was going on—the difficulty of the work, keeping pace with his own career—there was always the Dylan humor. It ran through everything he did. He sees the humorous and the ridiculous all about him and is quick to point it out, and, more often than not, creates his own—as when we approached Philadelphia on the way to a concert, and he "respectfully" donned his stove-pipe hat, in the best W. C. Fields tradition.

This humor is subtle and sometimes so disguised that it appears to be something else or almost goes unnoticed. It is present at interviews with the press when he plays upon words, and sometimes with the reporter himself. It appears in his songs, sometimes in songs that do not really present a humorous idea—and it is ourselves that we are laughing at. He is quick to respond to a joke or funny situation, but he is just as quick to fight the smile on his face, as if he did not want to be seen that way. This carried over into the way he saw himself in his pictures. When making selections, he usually chose those photographs in which he was serious or noncommital. Through his publicity pictures he could have created any kind of Dylan he wanted to. He chose to present a serious one, feeling intuitively that this was the best image for him at that time. But like everything else about Dylan, this could all change in an instant, and it wouldn't surprise me if one day he really does create a circus of his own, bringing to it all those things we have not yet seen.

At the Newport Folk Festival in the summer of 1965, Bob Dylan shocked his audience when he appeared on stage with an electric guitar, supported by other musicians who also used electrified instruments, and publicly performed the kind of music he had recorded on the "Bringing It All Back Home" album. A large block of the folk world present at that festival was up in arms. They booed and jeered at Newport, and many continued to do so afterward. For many, the high priest of the folk scene had desecrated the purity of folk music—and the greatest part of the insult was that he had done so on the hallowed ground of Newport.

When Dylan emerged from obscurity, the folk world said yes. When he brought to them new and brilliant material, the folk world said yes. When he proved himself as the man who was out front and capable of leading the way, the folk world again said yes. But when he dared to use the mantle of leadership to move one step beyond the conventional, many screamed *no*! The folk world was supposedly one of the rare places where freedom of thought and expression was allowed to flourish—a last stronghold; yet some of the people who held this freedom of thought attitude were the first to cast stones when Dylan explored a new area and freely expressed himself. Folk Rock is just one musical expression. Since its introduction, Dylan has produced other kinds of music. Dylan is not a follower, and he never took his rights from his audience. His strength and conviction come primarily from within, and as always, he was just making music. It's still all music and it's still all Dylan.

At the end of the summer, Dylan gave a concert at Forest Hills Stadium in New York City, where 14,000 people filled the stands to capacity. I arrived at the stadium before Dylan, so that I could acquaint myself with the photographic problems. The weather forecast called for showers, and this was still a matter for concern, since Forest Hills is an open stadium.

A huge horseshoe of seats faced the stage. Large wooden speaker enclosures stood at the edge of the lawn, facing the stands. The grounds were deserted except for some musicians and stage and production people standing about in conversation near the stage. A small group of fans had gathered near the gate hoping to meet Dylan and get his autograph. Shadows of clouds were sweeping across the field. The feeling that this entire place would in a few hours be pulsating with life was something everyone seemed aware of. As though a baton had been lifted, it all began when, about 2:00 p.m., Dylan arrived, accompanied by Albert Grossman.

Dylan stood about for a few minutes talking with his fans, and then with his musicians and production people, with whom he discussed the day's schedule. A light rain started to fall, and we decided that it was a good time to duck in somewhere and have some lunch. At the end of a long row of tennis courts we found the dining room of a tennis club.

While we had sandwiches, I asked how his book was coming along—the last time I had seen him, he had been working on *Tarantula*. He complained about the shortage of time that plagued him as more and more things were happening in his career. Record sessions, a book to be written, preparation for a TV show, concerts—all of these things were demanding his time. I don't have time for a lot of things anymore, he told me. Everyone wants me to do something. It was obvious that after his talent and energy, time was the next most important commodity, and the limit on that was fixed. What he seemed to be saying was, unfortunately we are all burdened with outside forces that restrict our freedom. He knew that he would have to give something up in order to make a compromise with this reality. The rain stopped and we all filed back to the stadium.

The preparation for this concert was unlike any other Dylan concert I had seen. In the past, Bob would bring his guitar, some harmonicas, and his small case of microphone equipment. On this day, things were approaching the conditions of a recording studio. There were many microphones to unpack, microphone stands to assemble, and dozens of coils of cable to unwind. The instruments had to be set up and arranged on stage. Microphones had to be placed and then balanced for sound. There were problems caused by the rustling sound made by the wind as it rushed by the mike heads. Voice levels had to be balanced so they could be heard over the sound of the instruments. It went on and on. Half a dozen people worked at it, and the musicians and Dylan were constantly needed for sound checks. It was an astonishing contrast to the preparation required for the first Dylan concert I attended almost a year earlier.

Albert Grossman personally supervised all of the setting up. He helped with every phase of the operation, and seemed to be everywhere at once, always with complete control over the situation. In order to be certain of the quality of the sound, he sat in the distant stands with a walkie-talkie radio unit, and guided the engineers in the sound booth until the microphones were properly set. Although he never tampers with the creative part of Dylan, he is a great support and guide for the incredible amount of work and planning that must go into the production of such an undertaking as Forest Hills or any concert of this size.

After a few hours of this kind of work, Dylan spent some time with the men who were going to play with him. Programming had to be discussed—problems the music would face in this particular stadium. Finally, all was done but the waiting. Night and the audience were on their way.

The stands were packed when the concert began. People had been arriving for hours. Some came in the late afternoon, took seats, and waited. Spotlights pierced the windy night when Dylan emerged from behind a canvas flap which was the stage entrance. The beams of light followed him to the microphone. There was a roar of applause as Dylan and his acoustical guitar began to sing. During the first part of the concert he performed as he always had—alone. It ended with overwhelming applause.

During the intermission Dylan held a conference with the musicians who were going to accompany him in the second half of the concert. He told them they should expect anything to happen—he probably was remembering what occurred at Newport. He told them that the audience might yell and boo, and that they should not be bothered by it. Their job, he said, was to make the best music they were capable of, and let whatever happened happen. He was aware of the possible reaction of his audience, but he was willing to risk that and stand with his convictions. The artist must be true to himself. He must be satisfied with what he produces—this is the prime factor in the production of his art. I always had great respect for this part of Dylan. He was always true to himself and produced what he believed was his best.

When Dylan appeared for the second half of the concert with an electric guitar, followed by musicians who occupied the stage with him, there was a sound of disapproval that rumbled from the stands. This was answered by the sound of the music coming from the large speakers in front of each section of seats. The twang of the electrified instruments shattered the night. The electric guitars, the pounding of the drums, and Dylan's wail rode the wind that swept across the open stadium, penetrating its farthest reaches. The music was Folk Rock in all its glory.

When the music started, the audience grew quiet. When it stopped, they would cry out, "We want Dylan! We want Dylan!" Boos were abundant, but when Dylan started a new number, there was quiet. This was the clue to it all—the audience had the right to disapprove, and they did, but at the same time they listened to the material. They were willing to give Dylan his chance. They respected him.

I have read an account that described objects hard and soft being thrown onto the stage and half of the audience becoming a mob. But it would have taken a major league ball player to throw any object onto the stage, considering the distance which separated it from the stands. A few people in the audience did make a run for the stage, one or two actually succeeded in mounting the platform. When they did, they seemed content just to run across. I asked one boy why he did this and he replied, "I just wanted to touch him." Dylan never stopped singing, he never broke his stride. He was doing just what he had told his quartet to do: Make the best music you can and don't be intimidated.

When he finished his last number, he put down his guitar and walked off. By not taking his instrument with him, it appeared that he was going to return for an encore. Instead, he went directly to a waiting car at the back gate. After much experience, it seemed a better plan to make a get-away seconds after leaving the stage than to wait out the crowds in the dressing room. Dylan had done this a number of times before the Forest Hills concert. It seemed a better thing to do than to create a situation in which some youngster would be crushed in a mob.

Bob Neuwirth, who was Dylan's road manager at the time of this concert, had asked me to set up the seats in the station wagon, but I didn't know how. I fought the problem to the last second, and just as I saw the two men running toward the car, I managed to get it up. Neuwirth dived behind the wheel, Bob leaped into the back seat and we sped away into a one-way street the wrong way. Crowds were pouring out of the·stadium—they were sure to spot us. Dylan huddled down. Neuwirth backed out of the street and aimed for Manhattan. During the trip back, Bob asked about the confusion on stage; he was worried someone might have gotten hurt. Then he wanted to know if the music he performed was his sound—Was it Dylan? This was his main concern. There was no doubt in my mind. Everything about it was Dylan.

Later, at the apartment of his manager, there was a gathering of some of Dylan's friends. Bob, relaxing in his stocking feet, asked a young lady who had been at the concert for her opinion of what she had seen and heard. She replied that she had no feelings. Finally, under some pressure, she admitted that she did not particularly like the new music. Asked if she had booed, she replied that she had not. Why not?

was Dylan's question. Why hadn't she made her feelings known? She would not answer. If you don't like something, you should let your feelings be known—you should have booed, Dylan told her. He was not telling her that she should have liked what he did, or that she should learn to like it, or that she didn't understand it. What he was telling her was that she should react, feel, and express herself. If there is a lesson, or a message, in Dylan's work, it is probably just that: We must respond as we see fit, and let our insides out. Every man has a right to be his own man, and he should be it. This is what Dylan's music is all about. It is a man expressing himself.

The following month, Dylan, wearing a beautifully tailored tweed suit, gave a concert at Carnegie Hall in New York City. Once again, the house was sold out. And once again, Dylan performed as he had done at Forest Hills. For the first half of his performance, he was alone with his acoustical guitar. For the second half, he appeared with his electric instrument and his quartet, and, as he did at Forest Hills, performed at the piano. But this time, the mood was different. His audience was beginning to understand his new music, and they showed it in their response. The tide had turned at Carnegie Hall and it was clear that it was only a matter of time before this sound would penetrate every place where popular music is performed. It was the same old story—Dylan was out in front with his message, and his ideas, and it would take a little time for everyone else to catch up.

Photography has brought me into contact with many notable people, including three Presidents of the United States, and I have happily had the opportunity to meet and talk with prominent people in all walks of life. Although many of these encounters were memorable, my association with Dylan has a special meaning. Dylan was not an aging philosopher who had, at long last, broken through the false billboard scenery about him, nor was he a scholar surrounded by walls covered with degrees. I met a man, who, although young, younger than I, could see the truth and the hypocrisy and false values around us. More than that, he was able to communicate this. This, more than anything else, drew me to him. The closer I got to Dylan, and the more I realized his talent and his potential, the more incredible it all became. And tomorrow, his talent and energy could take him in a hundred different directions. He himself may not yet have tested all of his abilities. What he has already produced is exceptional and wonderful. What he may yet produce is beyond what can be said here and now.

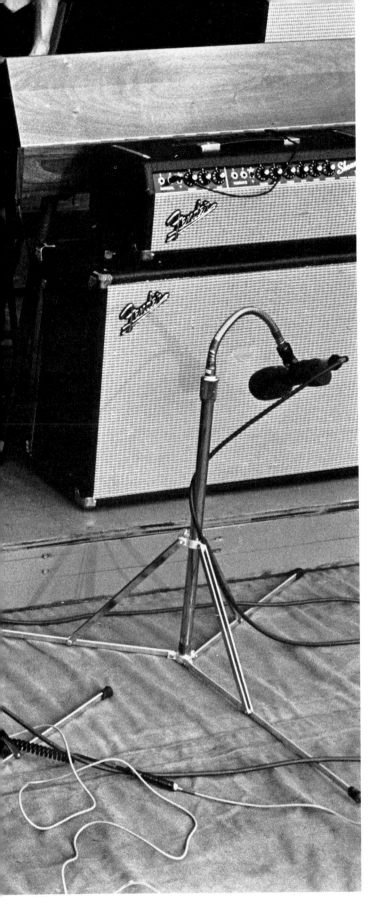

Daniel Kramer is a New York-based photographer and film director. After working as an assistant to Allan and Diane Arbus and Philipe Halsman, he opened his own studio. Kramer's portraits and picture stories have been widely published in national and international magazines. He also photographs for corporations and advertising agencies, and his work has been exhibited and collected by various museums. His photographs were featured on the album covers of *Bringing It All Back Home, Highway 61 Revisited*, and *Biograph*. For more than twenty years he has worked in association with his wife, Arline Cunningham.